FESTIVE SEAFOOD COOKERY

Compiled by Edna Beilenson
With Decorations by
Maggie Jarvis

—◆—

THE PETER PAUPER PRESS
MOUNT VERNON · NEW YORK

TO THE READER

Seafood, or "the fruit of the sea" as the French would have it, is particularly rewarding to serve, and is low in caloric content, — a boon to those who wish to watch their figures! It is rewarding because it can be cooked simply and quickly for week-a-day meals, or with very little effort can be converted into an unusual and delicious party food.

All that a good seafood dish really demands of the cook is that the fish be fresh! It would be nice if you could go out and catch the fish you serve, but this being impossible, alas, for the majority of us, let me beg of you to be careful where you buy your fish. Frozen seafood does very well, of course, and is much superior to "fresh" fish which is not-so-fresh. The delicate flavor of fish is ephemeral and short-lived, but it is worth every effort you can make to catch it — so shop carefully!

We hope you will enjoy the recipes in this little book, and will try those which are new to you so that your reputation as a good cook may be enhanced by the broadening of your menus. Adding your own little touches will make you feel truly creative. Have fun!

THE EDITOR

FESTIVE SEAFOOD COOKERY

BOUILLABAISSE

2 pounds firm-grained fish
  (whiting, haddock, eel, bass, etc.)
2 cups canned lobster
½ cup olive oil
3 cloves garlic, crushed
Rind of 1 orange
1 tomato, cut in two
Parsley, bay leaf, saffron, fennel
1½ quarts water

Cut fish (using several varieties) into 2-inch pieces. Add lobster.

In a large saucepan, place olive oil, a few sprigs of parsley, 1 or 2 bay leaves, the tomato, a pinch of saffron, a sprig of fennel, the orange rind and garlic. Add fish, cover with 1½ quarts water and bring to a boil. Boil quickly 15-20 minutes and remove pan from fire. Replace cooked limp parsley with a tablespoon of finely cut fresh parsley. Pour bouillabaisse into a

5

serving tureen over several thick slices of white bread. Serves 8-10.

GOURMET FISH SOUP

3 tablespoons olive oil
1 tablespoon garlic, minced
1 cup onion, finely chopped
2 teaspoons crumbled leaf saffron
½ teaspoon chopped fresh or dried thyme
1½ pounds flounder fillets
Salt and pepper
Tabasco sauce
1 cup dry white wine
4 cups water
⅓ cup tomato purée
1 teaspoon crushed fennel seeds
3 tablespoons Cognac
2 cups heavy cream

Heat the oil in a kettle and add the garlic, onion, saffron and thyme. Cook, stirring, until onion is golden brown. Add the fish, salt, pepper and Tabasco. Cook briefly, stirring to break up fish. Add the wine, water, tomato purée and fennel seeds. Bring to a boil and simmer 15 minutes, stirring occasionally. Add salt and pepper to taste and add the Cognac. Stir in cream and bring to a boil. Simmer 10 minutes. Serves 8 or more.

CRAB MEAT AND SHERRY SOUP

1 cup tomato soup
1 cup pea soup
1 cup crab meat, flaked
½ cup okra
1 tablespoon Sherry

Combine soups, okra, and crab meat. Heat together in top of double boiler, adding some water if necessary to thin. Add Sherry just before serving. Serves 4-6.

SALMON CASSEROLE

1 cup elbow macaroni
2 cups medium white sauce
1½ cups flaked salmon
3 cups cooked carrots and peas
½ cup grated American cheese

Cook macaroni in boiling, salted water 10 minutes, or until tender; place ½ of it in bottom of greased casserole, cover with salmon, and pour ½ of white sauce over fish. Place carrots, peas and remaining macaroni in layers on top, and pour remaining white sauce over all. Sprinkle top with cheese and bake in 350° oven 45 minutes. Serves 6.

SALMON WITH DILL WEED AND SOUR CREAM

Poach salmon in water seasoned with:

½ teaspoon seasoning salt
½ teaspoon shredded parsley
¼ teaspoon celery seed
1 teaspoon salt
Whole black pepper

and serve either hot or cold with the following sauce:

1 cup sour cream
1 teaspoon dill weed
1 tablespoon eschalot wine vinegar
¼ teaspoon sugar
1 teaspoon salt

SALMON SOUFFLÉ

4 tablespoons butter	1 cup milk
5 tablespoons flour	2 (7-oz.) cans salmon
½ teaspoon salt	6 eggs, separated

Melt butter, add flour and salt. Add milk gradually, stirring constantly. Cool and add the flaked salmon, and slightly beaten egg yolks. Fold in stiffly beaten egg whites and bake in buttered casserole at 300° for 1¼ hours. Serves 6.

FRESH SALMON MOUSSE

1 pound fresh salmon
½ envelope gelatin
2 tablespoons cold water
2 egg yolks
1 teaspoon salt
1 teaspoon prepared mustard
Few grains cayenne pepper
1½ tablespoons melted butter
¾ cup milk
2 tablespoons vinegar
Russian dressing

Cook salmon in slightly salted water to cover until tender, about 15 minutes. Do not overcook. Remove skin and bones and separate into large flakes. Cool. Soak gelatin in cold water for 5 minutes. Mix egg yolks with salt, mustard and cayenne. Add butter, milk and vinegar. Cook in top of double boiler over hot, not boiling, water, stirring constantly, until mixture is consistency of mayonnaise. Add dissolved gelatin and salmon. Turn into fish or other mold that has been dipped in cold water. Chill and allow to set for several hours or overnight. Serve with Russian dressing. Canned salmon may be used if fresh salmon is not available, and a little dill may be added if desired. Serves 4-6.

SALMON TARRAGON

3 pounds fresh salmon, in one piece
2 cups water
½ cup Tarragon wine vinegar
1 tablespoon instant minced onions
4 whole black peppercorns
Salt
Pepper

Place salmon on rack in large kettle. Combine water, vinegar, salt and pepper, onions, and peppercorns; pour over fish. Cover and simmer over low heat about 45 minutes. Lift fish out carefully; remove skin. Serve either hot or well chilled. Arrange salmon on platter and top servings of salmon with spoonfuls of Tarragon Sauce (below). Serves 6 for dinner or 8 for luncheon.

Tarragon Sauce:

1 cup sour cream
2 tablespoons Tarragon white wine vinegar
Salt and pepper
1 tablespoon cut scallions
½ teaspoon sugar

Combine sour cream, vinegar, salt and pepper, scallions, and sugar. Decorate the salmon with parsley, if desired.

11

STRIPED BASS, CHINESE STYLE

3 tablespoons vegetable oil
1 pound boneless fillets of fresh striped bass,
    cut into ½ -inch strips
¼ cup minced scallion
½ cup diagonally sliced celery pieces
½ cup bamboo shoots
½ cup sliced water chestnuts
½ cup sliced small mushrooms
⅓ cup fish or chicken stock
½ teaspoon salt
1 teaspoon soy sauce
1 teaspoon Accent
1 teaspoon cornstarch
1 tablespoon water

Heat two tablespoons oil in heavy skillet. Over medium high heat, rapidly stir-fry fish pieces, turning with wooden spoon until cooked, about one minute on each side. Remove fish from pan and keep warm. Add remaining oil to skillet and over high heat cook scallions, celery, bamboo shoots, water chestnuts and mushrooms quickly, stirring, one minute. Add fish stock, salt, soy sauce and Accent. Cover and boil five minutes. Mix cornstarch with water and add along with pieces of fish to skillet. Stir and heat just until mixture thickens. Serves 4.

FILLET OF SOLE, GRAPES AND MUSHROOMS

3 pounds fillet of sole
2 cups milk
¼ cup butter
1 pound sliced mushrooms
2 cups skinned seedless grapes
4 tablespoons butter
8 tablespoons flour
1 teaspoon salt
¼ teaspoon pepper
½ teaspoon celery salt
½ cup buttered bread crumbs
¼ cup Parmesan cheese, grated

Cover fillet of sole with milk and cook over low heat 5 minutes. Drain, reserving milk. Melt ¼ cup butter; add mushrooms and cook 5 minutes. Mix together mushrooms and grapes; place in casserole. Place fish over mushrooms and grapes. Melt 4 tablespoons butter. Blend in flour. Add reserved milk gradually, stirring constantly. Continue stirring and cook over low heat until thick. Add salt and pepper and celery salt. Pour sauce over fish. Sprinkle bread crumbs and cheese over top of casserole. Bake in 400° oven about ½ hour. Serves 8.

FILLET OF SOLE AU GRATIN

6 fillets of sole
½ onion, chopped
2 tablespoons butter
12 mushrooms
Lemon juice
1 teaspoon chopped parsley
½ cup tomato sauce
Salt and pepper
2 tablespoons bread crumbs
½ wine-glass of white wine

Put onions and 1 tablespoon butter in a saucepan and cook a few minutes. Slice 6 mushrooms and cook about 5 minutes in a very little cold water with a few drops lemon juice, then put them aside to serve around fish. Chop stems and remaining mushrooms and add to butter and onions. Cover and cook until water from mushrooms is just cooked away. Add a little chopped parsley and tomato sauce, and boil a few minutes. Spread bottom of an ovenproof serving dish with some of this sauce and place fillets, seasoned with salt and pepper, on the sauce. Drain cooked mushrooms, place on fillets, and cover with remaining sauce. Sprinkle with bread crumbs and remaining tablespoon butter (melted) and wine. Place in 350° oven, and bake 12 to 15 minutes. Remove from oven and sprinkle with a little lemon juice and remaining parsley. Serves 6.

FILLETS IN MUSHROOM WINE SAUCE

4 tablespoons butter
1 onion, chopped fine
1 green pepper, chopped fine
¼ pound mushrooms, sliced
1 cup clam juice
¼ teaspoon salt
⅛ teaspoon pepper
½ cup dry white wine
1½ lbs. fillet of sole or flounder (four fillets)

Melt the butter and add the finely chopped onion and green pepper; sauté until onion is soft. Add the sliced mushrooms and sauté briefly, until slices are slightly browned around the edges. Add the clam juice, salt, pepper and white wine. Simmer gently for 10 minutes. Arrange the fish fillets in a single layer in a greased shallow baking dish. Spoon mushrooms in sauce carefully over each fillet and bake in a 400° oven for 15 to 20 minutes or until fish flakes easily. Serves 4 generously.

STUFFED FISH FILLETS

6 fillets of flounder
3 cups toasted bread cubes
⅓ cup melted butter
1 cup applesauce
2 tablespoons grated lemon rind
1 small onion, chopped
2 tablespoons parsley, chopped
1 teaspoon salt
1 teaspoon Angostura aromatic bitters
Paprika

Combine all ingredients except fillets and paprika. Place 1/6th of filling mixture on one end of each fillet. Roll fillets around stuffing. Fasten with toothpick. Place on a foil-lined greased baking pan, sprinkle with paprika, and bake at 375° for 15-20 minutes or until fish flakes. Serves 6.

LEMON SOLE WITH RED CAVIAR

6 lemon sole fillets   Soft butter
6 tablespoons red caviar   Salt and pepper

The red caviar may be mixed with soft butter, or 1 teaspoonful may be spread on each fillet with a liberal spreading of soft butter. Roll the fillets and fasten with skewers. Stand the rolls on end, close together, in a well-buttered casserole. Cover tightly and bake about 18 minutes at 350°. Uncover the casserole for the last 5 minutes. Sprinkle a little salt and ground pepper over the top of the fillets. Serve a little pan sauce over each fillet.

FILLET OF SOLE SOUR CREAM

1 large onion	Salt and pepper
3 tablespoons butter	8 small fillets of sole
4 tomatoes, sliced	1 pint sour cream

Slice onion very thin. Melt butter in flat baking dish and sauté onion until golden. Cook sliced tomatoes separately a few minutes and spread on top of onion. Salt and pepper fish on both sides and lay on top of tomatoes. Broil, dotted with butter, a few minutes until brown on top. Pour on sour cream and return to broiler until top is brown in patches. Serves 4.

TROUT AMANDINE

3 pounds trout fillets
½ cup butter
¼ cup sliced blanched almonds
2 tablespoons lemon juice
1 teaspoon chopped parsley

Rinse trout; pat dry with paper towels. Heat ¼ cup butter in large skillet until very hot. Add fillets, and brown on each side, about 3 minutes per side. Remove to warm platter; keep warm. Add remaining butter to skillet; heat. Add almonds; sauté until well browned. Stir in lemon juice. Pour over trout. Sprinkle with parsley. Serves 4.

SHAD ROE À LA FRANCAISE

2 large pairs shad roe
½ pound sorrel leaves
Salt and pepper
4 tablespoons butter
6 scallions, chopped
1 cup dry white wine
1½ cups heavy cream

Wash and dry the roe. Stem the sorrel leaves and chop them finely in a wooden bowl. Add salt and pepper. Melt the butter in a pan, add the chopped scallions and the roe. Cook gently for 1 minute, then add the wine and sorrel leaves. Cook very slowly for 20 minutes, carefully turning the roe after they have cooked 10 minutes. Lift the roe onto a serving dish and keep hot. Add cream to the sauce and reduce it by cooking 5 minutes. Pour the sauce over the roe and serve. Serves 4.

BAKED HALIBUT IN SPANISH SAUCE

6 tablespoons olive oil
4 halibut steaks (4-6 oz. each)
1 medium onion, minced
1 clove garlic, minced
¼ cup parsley, minced
1 large tomato, skinned and chopped
¾ teaspoon salt
1 teaspoon sugar
2 tablespoons tomato paste
½ cup dry Sherry
½ cup water
4 lemon slices

Preheat oven to 350°. Spoon two tablespoons oil over bottom of shallow baking dish. Place fish steaks in the oil. Heat remaining oil in a heavy skillet and sauté onion, garlic and parsley until yellow and soft, 15 to 20 minutes. Add tomato, salt and sugar and continue cooking until well blended. Add tomato paste, Sherry and water and simmer five minutes longer. Pour over fish. Place a lemon slice atop each steak and brush lightly with olive oil to keep moist. Bake 30 minutes or until fish flakes easily, spooning sauce over a few times during cooking. Serve garnished with ripe black olives, parsley and sliced tomatoes. Serves 4.

HALIBUT BAKED IN SOUR CREAM

1 pound fresh halibut fillets
1 cup sour cream
⅛ teaspoon mustard
⅛ teaspoon ginger
¼ teaspoon salad herbs
Paprika, salt and pepper

Arrange fish fillets in flat baking dish. Mix together mustard, ginger, salt, salad herbs and pepper and blend into sour cream. Spread over fish. Sprinkle with paprika. Bake in a 400° oven for 30 minutes or until fish is done and sauce bubbly. Serve at once. Serves 4.

BAKED WHITE FISH

Whole whitefish
3 stalks celery, diced small
2 large onions, diced small
1 (#2½) can tomatoes
2 tablespoons butter
Salt, pepper, Accent, paprika

Have fish split in half and each half cut into 3 pieces. Wash in cold running water and dry each piece. Place in greased, shallow baking dish. Sprinkle lightly with salt, pepper, Accent and paprika. Scatter celery and onion over fish. Mash tomatoes and pour entire contents of can over fish. Dot each piece with butter, sprinkle lightly with paprika. Bake at 350° for 1 hour. Serves 6.

SOUFFLÉ OF FISH

1 cup cooked fish
  (cod, halibut, or other white fish)
3 tablespoons butter
3 tablespoons flour
1½ cups milk
3 egg yolks, beaten
½ teaspoon salt
Pepper
4 egg whites, stiffly beaten

Chop fish very fine and run through a coarse sieve. Melt butter, add flour, and cook until it just starts to turn golden. Add milk and cook, stirring constantly, until mixture thickens. Continue cooking gently, stirring occasionally, until reduced to about 1 cup. Combine with egg yolks by mixing a little of the sauce to the yolks and then turning this back into the sauce. Cook over a very low heat, stirring vigorously until it just starts to boil. Remove from fire and add salt, pepper, and fish. Fold in stiffly beaten egg whites. Turn into a buttered and floured soufflé dish, and bake at 450° for 15 to 20 minutes. Serve immediately. Serves 4.

FISH SALAD LOAF

1 cup cottage cheese
1 cup mayonnaise
½ teaspoon ginger
2 tablespoons lemon juice
2 drops Tabasco sauce
2 tablespoons gelatin
¼ cup cold water
1 cup fish, flaked
⅓ cup ripe olives, sliced
1 cup carrot, shredded
½ cup celery, finely cut
4 tablespoons pepper relish
1 teaspoon salt

Whip the cottage cheese and combine with the mayonnaise, adding the ginger, lemon juice and Tabasco sauce. Soak the gelatin in the cold water and then dissolve it over boiling water. Blend it with the mayonnaise. Mix the remaining ingredients and combine the two mixtures. Pour into loaf pan or ring mold and chill. Unmold and garnish with salad greens and ripe olives. Salmon, tuna, whitefish, or any firm leftover fish may be used. Serves 4.

FISH MOUSSE

1 tablespoon gelatin
3 tablespoons lemon juice
2 cups hot clam bouillon
1 cup flaked canned fish or crab meat
1 cup celery, finely cut
1 pimento, finely cut
½ cup thick sour cream
1 tablespoon horseradish
½ teaspoon dry mustard
½ teaspoon salt

Dissolve the gelatin in the hot clam bouillon. Add lemon juice and chill. When almost firm, beat until frothy with egg beater. Whip the sour cream, blending in the salt, mustard and horseradish. Mix the remaining ingredients and fold into the gelatin mixture, then add the sour cream. Chill until firm in a loaf or ring mold. Serve on lettuce. Serves 4.

CRAB MEAT ROYALE

6 cups mashed potatoes
3 cups flaked crab meat
¾ cup buttered crumbs
1½ cups medium white sauce

Line casserole with mashed potatoes; bake in 400° oven 10 minutes, or until slightly browned. Fill with combined crab meat and white sauce. Sprinkle with crumbs and return dish to oven for 15 minutes. Garnish with parsley. Serves 8.

CRAB MEAT QUICHE

1½ cups crab meat
1 tablespoon celery, chopped
1 tablespoon onion, chopped
2 tablespoons parsley, chopped
2 tablespoons Sherry
Pastry for one 9″ pie crust
4 eggs, lightly beaten
2 cups light cream
¼ teaspoon nutmeg
½ teaspoon salt
¼ teaspoon pepper

Pick over crab meat to remove bits of shell and cartilage. Combine with celery, onion, parsley and Sherry and refrigerate 1 hour. Preheat oven to 450°. Line pie plate with pastry and bake 5 minutes. Place crab meat mixture in partly baked pie shell. Combine eggs, cream, nutmeg, salt and pepper and pour over crab meat. Bake 15 minutes at 450°, reduce temperature to 350°, and bake about 10 minutes longer, until a knife inserted in center of pie comes out clean. Serves 8.

CRAB CAKES MARYLAND

2 (14-oz.) cans fresh crab meat
3 ounces sweet butter
2 medium onions, chopped
1 green pepper, chopped
2 tablespoons flour
2 cups hot milk
1 egg
1 dash Tabasco sauce
Salt and pepper to taste
1 teaspoon dry mustard
½ teaspoon parsley, chopped
Flour, cracker meal, beaten egg

Pick over crab meat to remove cartilage. Sauté onion and green pepper lightly in butter. Add flour, stir till smooth, then hot milk and 1 egg, stirring constantly. Add seasonings and parsley. Cook over low heat for 10 minutes. Remove from heat, fold in crab meat. Cool. Mold into 12 flat cakes. Dip in flour, then beaten egg, then cracker meal. Fry in deep hot fat, 400°, until golden brown. Serve with shrimp sauce (below). Serves 6.

Shrimp Sauce:

Sauté 1 cup cut-up shrimp in butter. Add a little Sherry, combine with 1 cup cream sauce. Heat but do not boil.

CRAB MEAT CASSEROLE

2 cups crab meat
6 hard-boiled eggs, sliced
½ pound sautéed mushrooms
1½ cups cream sauce
½ cup grated Parmesan cheese
3 tablespoons Sherry
¾ cup walnut meats, halved
Salt, pepper

Stir grated cheese, Sherry, salt, and pepper into cream sauce and simmer gently. Butter baking dish, and alternate layers of crab, eggs, mushrooms and walnuts. Cover with sauce and top with bread crumbs and additional grated cheese. Bake at 350° for about 1 hour. Serves 6.

DEVILLED CRABS

1 tablespoon butter
1 tablespoon flour
1 cup milk
Pinch salt
¼ teaspoon paprika
1 teaspoon parsley, chopped
¼ cup Swiss cheese, grated
½ pound crab meat
1 egg, beaten
Bread crumbs

Melt butter, add flour, stir until smooth,

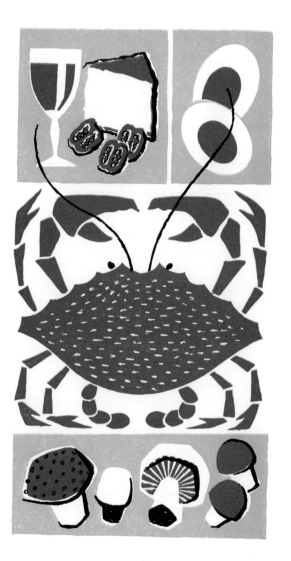

add milk gradually and stir until slightly thickened. Add salt, paprika, parsley and Swiss cheese. Stir until cheese is melted and sauce thick and creamy. Add crab meat and egg. Place in shells, sprinkle with bread crumbs and paprika, and dot with butter. Bake in 450° oven 25 to 30 minutes or until browned. Serves 5.

CHINESE BRAISED SHRIMP

1 pound medium sized shelled shrimp
6 cooked water chestnuts, cut into
   small squares
4 cooked mushrooms, cut into small pieces
½ cup canned peas
2 slices thinly sliced ham, cut into
   small squares
1 piece powdered ginger
1 scallion head, chopped fine
1 teaspoon salt
2 teaspoons cornstarch
2 teaspoons soy sauce
2 teaspoons white wine
1 teaspoon cooking oil
⅓ cup vegetable shortening
1 cup chicken or fish stock

Heat shortening in frying pan. Sauté the shrimp gently with the ginger, onion, soy sauce, wine, stock and salt. Add water chestnuts, mushrooms, peas and ham separately. Mix cornstarch with a little cold water and add to mixture. Finally add the cooking oil and sauté about three minutes. Serves 4.

FROGS' LEGS MEUNIÈRE

2 pounds frogs' legs
Milk
Flour
Oil
Lemon juice
Chopped parsley
Lemon wedges

Clean frogs' legs, cut off the feet, and soak in cold water two hours. Drain and dry well. Dip in milk, then in flour, and sauté slowly in hot oil about 6 to 8 minutes (depending upon size), or until brown on all sides. Put in serving dish and season with salt, pepper, and a few drops of lemon juice. Pour off the oil from the pan and add butter, allowing one-half tablespoon for each person. Cook until brown in color and pour over frogs' legs. Sprinkle with chopped parsley and garnish with a wedge of lemon for each serving. For parties, slice and scallop lemon. Serves 4.

FROGS' LEGS POULETTE

2 pounds frogs' legs
½ pound mushrooms
2 tablespoons butter
1 tablespoon onion, chopped
½ cup top milk
½ wine-glass of white wine
1 teaspoon flour
½ teaspoon salt
Pepper
1 teaspoon parsley, chopped

Wash frogs' legs, cut off feet, and soak in cold water two hours. Drain and dry well. Clean and chop mushrooms and put in a saucepan with 1 tablespoon butter, onions, and frogs' legs. Add wine, bring to a boil, and cook 10 to 12 minutes. Remove frogs' legs to serving dish. Cook liquid in pan until reduced to not more than ¼ cup. Add top milk, bring back to the boil, and cook 2 to 3 minutes. Thicken sauce with Manié Butter, made by creaming together remaining butter and flour and adding to the liquid. Bring to a boil, stirring constantly. Add parsley, and pour over frogs' legs. Serve with delicately sautéed small whole potatoes and green peas. Serves 4.

TEMPTING TUNA ORIENTAL

1⅓ cups (9¼-oz. can) tuna, drained
½ cup (4-oz. can) sliced mushrooms, drained
1½ cups chow mein noodles
1 cup celery, chopped
½ cup cashew nuts, sliced
2 cups sour cream
Salt

Preheat oven to 350°. Combine tuna, mushrooms, noodles, celery and cashews (reserve a few for garnish) with sour cream; salt to taste. Place in baking dish and bake 20 minutes. Garnish with reserved cashews and some noodles. If desired, remaining noodles may be heated slightly and passed separately. Serves 6.

CLAM FRITTERS

2 cups canned clams
2 eggs, beaten
1 cup sour milk

2 cups flour
1 teaspoon soda
½ teaspoon salt

Put the clam meat through a food chopper. Add to the beaten eggs, then add sour milk, salt and soda sifted with the flour. Blend well after each addition. If the batter is too thick, add a little clam juice. Drop by small spoonfuls into deep fat and fry until well browned. Serves 6.

HERRING AND POTATO CASSEROLE

1 pound salt herring
6 boiled potatoes, sliced
2 onions, sliced
¼ cup soft bread crumbs
2 tablespoons butter

Soak herring overnight; drain and cut into bits, removing entrails and as many bones as possible. Place herring, potatoes and onions in layers in greased casserole, beginning and ending with potatoes; sprinkle with bread crumbs and dot with butter. Bake in 425° oven ½ hour, or until nicely browned. Serves 6.

SEAFOOD CURRY CASSEROLE

4 tablespoons butter
4 tablespoons flour
2 cups milk
1 teaspoon salt
1 teaspoon curry powder
2 cups cooked peas
2 cups flaked fish (haddock, halibut, whitefish, salmon)
16 shrimp
3 hard-boiled eggs, chopped
Grated cheese

Prepare white sauce of butter, flour, milk and seasonings. Add fish, peas, shrimp and chopped eggs. Grease casserole, sprinkle with cheese. Bake until brown. Serves 8.

SCALLOPS AND EGGS

2 pounds scallops
3 hard-boiled eggs
1 cup fine crumbs
2 cups cream sauce
½ cup green pepper, diced
½ cup celery, diced
2 tablespoons grated cheese

Rinse and drain scallops; cover with cold water, heat slowly to boiling and drain. Line a greased casserole with a thin layer of bread crumbs. Add scallops and sliced eggs in layers, sprinkling each layer with salt and finely diced green pepper and celery. Add cream sauce. Top with remaining crumbs, mixed with cheese, and bake in 350° oven 30 minutes. Serves 6.

MUSSELS MARINIÈRE

4 dozen mussels
4 shallots, chopped
2 wine-glasses of
  white wine
1 teaspoon flour
4 tablespoons butter
2 teaspoons chopped
  parsley

Clean mussels thoroughly. Put in a saucepan with shallots and wine. Cook about

6 to 8 minutes or until they open. Remove from pan and take off one shell from each mussel. Place in serving dish. Reduce the cooking liquor to ⅓ the original quantity and thicken with butter and flour which have been creamed together. Correct seasoning, add parsley and pour over the mussels. This is a gourmet dish, and suitable for party fare. Serves 4.

SCALLOP CASSEROLE

1 pound scallops, cut, if large
2 tablespoons butter, melted
¼ cup parsley, chopped
2 cups cooked green beans, cut
3 hard-boiled eggs, sliced
1 cup sour cream
1 cup American cheese, grated
¼ cup onion, finely minced

Sauté scallops in butter mixed with parsley until lightly browned on all sides. Place scallops and butter in 1½ quart casserole. Cover with layer of beans and layer of egg slices. Combine sour cream, cheese and onion, and spoon over egg. Cover and bake 15 minutes in 375° oven, till sauce is bubbly. Serve with rice and broiled tomatoes. Serves 4.

SHRIMP AND MUSHROOM CURRY

¾ cup flour
7 teaspoons curry powder
4 teaspoons salt
½ teaspoon ginger
2 teaspoons sugar
1½ cups minced onions
1½ cups sliced apples
¾ cup butter
1 quart chicken broth
2 cups milk
4 tablespoons butter
3 pounds cleaned, shelled shrimp
1½ pounds washed mushroom caps
¼ cup melted butter
2 tablespoons lemon juice
2 cups uncooked rice

On the day before, combine flour, curry powder, salt, ginger and sugar. Sauté onion and apple in ¾ cup butter until tender; blend in flour mixture. Slowly stir in chicken broth and milk; cook, stirring often, until thick. Remove from heat. In large skillet, melt 4 tablespoons butter; add shrimp, and sauté over high heat, stirring with fork, 5 minutes; drain. Add to curry sauce. Place mushroom caps in shallow pan; brush with 2 tablespoons melted butter; broil 3 minutes. Turn; brush with

2 tablespoons butter; broil 3 minutes longer. Add, with lemon juice, to curry sauce. Refrigerate. About ½ hour before serving: Cook 2 cups white rice as package directs. Reheat curry and serve over rice. Makes 8 servings.

SHRIMP CURRY

1 pound fresh shrimp
2 cups shrimp stock
2 chicken-bouillon cubes
½ tablespoon curry powder
Salt, pepper
2 tablespoons flour
2 tablespoons butter
2 cups hot, cooked rice
2 hard-boiled eggs

Cook and prepare shrimp, saving stock. To 2 cups strained shrimp stock, add bouillon cubes, and stir until dissolved; moisten curry powder with a little water and add to stock with salt and pepper, mixing well. Stir flour into melted butter; gradually stir in seasoned stock and cook over low heat until smooth and slightly thickened; then add shrimp. Mix shrimp and sauce with hot rice and cook 15 minutes; garnish with sliced eggs. Serves 4 generously.

HOT SHRIMP COCKTAIL

½ cup onion, chopped
1½ tablespoons butter
1¾ cups canned tomatoes
½ cup green pepper, chopped
⅓ cup salted crackers, crumbled
1 teaspoon salt
⅛ teaspoon pepper
Dash Worcestershire sauce
Nutmeg
⅛ teaspoon thyme
⅛ teaspoon mace
1 pound raw shrimp
1 egg, hard-boiled

Sauté finely chopped onion in butter until amber in color but not brown. Stir in canned tomatoes, chopped green pepper and crumbled salted crackers. Add salt, pepper, a dash of Worcestershire sauce, nutmeg, thyme and mace. Simmer for 15 minutes, stirring now and then. Shell and devein 1 pound raw shrimp. Add them to the sauce and simmer about 3 minutes. (Never use cooked shrimp). Chop a hard-boiled egg and stir it in last. Spoon into individual scallop shells, or a 1½-quart casserole. Bake in a moderate oven, 350°, for 15 minutes. Sprinkle with chopped hard-boiled egg if desired. Serves 6.

PAELLA

1 pound shrimp, cooked, shelled
12 Cherrystone clams
1 frying chicken (2½ lbs. ready to cook)
¼ cup flour
1 teaspoon salt
⅛ teaspoon pepper
2 tablespoons olive oil
2 tablespoons peanut oil
4 onions, finely chopped
2 green peppers, finely chopped
2 cloves garlic, crushed
3 tablespoons butter
1 cup rice
Spanish thread saffron
1¼ cups chicken broth
1 teaspoon Accent
1 can chick peas
1 package frozen green peas, cooked

Cut chicken for frying; sprinkle with seasoned flour. Heat the olive oil and peanut oil in a 12-inch skillet; brown chicken thoroughly, add ¼ cup water and cook until tender, approximately 20 minutes. Remove chicken. To drippings in pan add chopped onion, green pepper and garlic; cook over low heat until wilted. In a 1-quart saucepan melt butter, add unwashed rice and saffron; stir over low heat a few minutes. Add enough water to chicken stock to make 2¼ cups, stir in Accent and add to rice. Bring to boil; cook, covered, over low heat until rice is tender and liquid absorbed. Stir rice, chick peas and cooked green peas into onion mixture in skillet. Layer with chicken, shrimp, and clams in a 4-quart shallow casserole (or 2 smaller casseroles). Reserve a few clams for top. Bake in 350° oven for 15 minutes, or until clams open. Serve at once. Serves 6-8.

Note: Before using clams, soak in ice-cold salted water 1 hour; scrub with stiff brush; rinse under cold running water, and refrigerate until used.

SWEET AND PUNGENT SHRIMP

¼ cup brown sugar
2 tablespoons cornstarch
½ teaspoon salt
¼ cup vinegar
1 tablespoon soy sauce
1 green pepper, cut into strips
2 small onions, cut into rings
1 (#2) can pineapple chunks
1 pound shrimp, cooked and cleaned

Combine in saucepan brown sugar, cornstarch, salt, vinegar, soy sauce and syrup from canned pineapple. Cook until slightly thickened, stirring constantly. Add green pepper, onion and pineapple chunks and cook 2 or 3 minutes. Remove from heat, add shrimp and let stand about 10 minutes. Before serving, bring to a boil, stirring constantly. Serve on rice.

SEAFOOD CASSEROLE

2 cans frozen shrimp soup
2 tablespoons Sherry
2 small cans button mushrooms, drained
¼ cup slivered almonds
½ pound fresh lump crab meat
½ pound fresh shrimp, cooked and deveined
4 to 6 slices American cheese
Paprika

Defrost soup. Place in 2-quart casserole and stir in Sherry, mushrooms and almonds. Fold in seafood gently and cover with layer of sliced cheese. Sprinkle paprika over cheese. Refrigerate until ready to bake. Mixture is better when allowed to blend several hours. Bake, uncovered, in 300° oven for 1 hour. Serve over hot, fluffy rice. Lobster meat, or well-drained frozen seafood, may be substituted. Serves 4 generously.

CREOLE JAMBALAYA

2 tablespoons butter
½ cup chopped onion
1 clove garlic, crushed
¼ pound cooked ham, diced (¾ cup)
1 can (1 lb.) tomatoes, undrained
¾ cup canned condensed chicken broth
1½ pounds raw shrimp, shelled and deveined
1 tablespoon parsley, chopped
1 bay leaf
1 teaspoon salt
¼ teaspoon dried thyme leaves
½ teaspoon Tabasco
⅛ teaspoon pepper
1 cup raw long-grain white rice

Preheat oven to 350°. In hot butter in Dutch oven, sauté onion until soft — about 5 minutes. Add garlic and ham; sauté 5 minutes longer. Stir in tomatoes, chicken broth, shrimp, parsley, bay leaf, salt, thyme, Tabasco, and pepper. Bring to boiling, covered. Pour into a 2-quart casserole. Sprinkle rice over top of mixture; gently press into liquid just until rice is covered. Do not stir. Cover. Bake 40 minutes, or until rice is tender and liquid is absorbed. Toss gently before serving. With a mixed green salad, this makes an excellent meal. Serves 6.

SEAFOOD MOLD

1 package lemon gelatin
1 cup hot tomato juice
¼ cup white vinegar
1 teaspoon prepared mustard
⅓ cup white horseradish
2 tablespoons sweet pickle relish
2 tablespoons ketchup
Dash of Tabasco
1 pound cooked shrimp or other seafood
⅓ cup sour cream (optional)

Dissolve gelatin in hot tomato juice. Blend in all ingredients except shrimp. Refrigerate. When almost jelled, add shrimp. If desired, sour cream may be beaten in just before adding shrimp. Pour into 1-quart mold. Refrigerate for several hours until set. Unmold and garnish as desired. Serves 4.

OYSTERS TERRAPIN

1 pint oysters	Salt and pepper
1 pound mushrooms	1 recipe white sauce
3 onions, fried in butter	Toast

Add mushrooms to the onions which have been sliced fine and fried until light brown, and cook for about 15 minutes.

Season with salt and pepper. Combine with 1 pint of raw oysters, drained, and 1 standard recipe of white sauce. Cook gently a few minutes and serve on toast.

OYSTERS TETRAZZINI

3 dozen oysters
½ pound fine noodles
8 tablespoons butter
1 cup soft bread crumbs
¼ cup grated Parmesan cheese
¼ cup flour
2 teaspoons salt
⅛ teaspoon pepper
2 teaspoons Worcestershire sauce
3 cups milk
¼ cup Sherry
½ teaspoon salt
⅛ teaspoon pepper
½ teaspoon paprika

Drain oysters, reserving ½ cup liquid. Refrigerate oysters. Cook noodles, as package directs, until barely tender; drain; rinse; place in casserole; refrigerate. Melt butter in double boiler; remove 4 tablespoons, and mix with bread crumbs and cheese; refrigerate. To remaining butter, add flour and next 3 ingredients; slowly stir in reserved oyster liquid, milk. Cook, stirring often, until smooth and thick. Stir in Sherry; refrigerate. When ready to start baking, arrange oysters on top of noodles; sprinkle with ½ teaspoon salt, ⅛ teaspoon pepper, and paprika. Pour on sauce; top with crumb mixture. Bake 1 hour in 400° oven. Serves 8.

OYSTERS AND NOODLES

1 package (12-oz.) frozen oysters
¼ cup butter
Salt, pepper
½ teaspoon paprika
2½ tablespoons flour
1½ cups milk
2 cups uncooked broken noodles
½ cup buttered bread crumbs

Thaw oysters slightly. Sauté oysters in butter about 10 minutes, then add seasonings; remove oysters and stir flour into mixture in pan. Gradually add milk, stirring until thick and smooth. Cook noodles in rapidly boiling salted water about 10 minutes, or until tender; drain and arrange half of them in greased casserole. Cover with oysters, then add remaining noodles. Pour sauce over top and sprinkle with crumbs; bake in 450° oven 15 minutes. Serves 6.

GOURMET OYSTERS

4½ dozen oysters
2 cups evaporated milk
2 tablespoons butter
Salt, pepper
Grated rind of 1 lemon
1 cup grated Swiss cheese
1 tablespoon cornstarch
1 tablespoon cold water
Flour, seasoned with salt and pepper
3 eggs, slightly beaten
Toasted bread crumbs
1 cup crushed cornflakes

Carefully drain oysters and save 1 cup of oyster liquor for the following sauce: Chop fine 1 dozen of the oysters. Then heat with liquor, milk, butter, salt, pepper and lemon rind. Stir in cheese and thicken with a paste made of cornstarch and water. Dredge remaining oysters with seasoned flour. Dip in beaten eggs, roll in crumbs. Put a layer of oysters in a greased casserole. Cover with the sauce, sprinkle lightly with bread crumbs. Repeat layers, ending with sauce on top. Sprinkle with cornflakes, dot with butter. Bake in a 400° oven until thoroughly heated. Brown under broiler, watching carefully to avoid burning. Serves 8.

OYSTER CASSEROLE

1 cup mushrooms, sliced
8 tablespoons butter
1 cup fine crumbs
2 pints oysters
1 cup milk
½ cup light cream

Sauté sliced mushrooms in 2 tablespoons butter for 2 minutes. Line bottom of greased casserole with ⅓ of crumbs, add a layer of sliced mushrooms and dot with 1 tablespoon butter; add another layer of crumbs, then oysters, remaining sliced mushrooms and a final layer of crumbs. Pour milk, cream and remaining 5 tablespoons butter, melted, over top. Bake in 350° oven 25 minutes. Serves 6.

OYSTERS AND MACARONI

2½ dozen oysters
4 cups shell macaroni (8-oz.)
1 teaspoon salt
¼ teaspoon pepper
½ teaspoon paprika
½ pound sharp Cheddar cheese, grated
8 tablespoons melted butter
1 cup soft bread crumbs

Drain oysters, reserving ½ cup liquid. Cook macaroni until barely tender; drain and rinse. In a large baking dish, arrange a third of macaroni, then half of oysters. Sprinkle with half of salt, pepper, and paprika; one third of cheese; then 3 table-spoons butter. Repeat. Spread rest of macaroni on top. Pour on oyster liquid. Top with remaining butter tossed with crumbs; then sprinkle on remaining cheese. Refrigerate for 6 to 8 hours. Bake 30 minutes in 400° oven. Serves 10.

PANCAKES, STUFFED WITH LOBSTER HASH

Pancakes:

2 cups flour
½ teaspoon salt
1 teaspoon sugar
3 eggs
2¾ cups milk
1 tablespoon brandy
Butter

The pancakes should be made at least 3 hours before serving time, and may very well be made the day before. Sift the flour with salt and sugar. Break the eggs into a hole in the center of the flour, add ¾ cup milk and stir until smooth. Then gradual-ly add 2 more cups of milk and the brandy.

Fry in skillet which has been heated, sprinkled with salt and scoured with tissue paper, which will prevent sticking. Put a lump of butter into the hot pan, melt, pour in a little batter and tilt pan so that a thin film of batter covers the bottom of the pan. When the crepe is brown, flip it over and brown the other side. Spread the finished pancakes on wax paper until ready to use.

Lobster Filling:

1 large lobster
1 pound mushrooms
3 white onions
3 teaspoons flour
1 cup hot sweet cream
1 wine-glass Sherry
Butter

Boil and remove meat from the lobster, and put it through the meat grinder. Then put 1 pound mushrooms, stems and all, through the grinder. Sauté the mushrooms in butter until almost dry. Brown the onions, which have been sliced, in 2 tablespoons butter. Remove onions from butter and add the ground lobster which has been sprinkled with the flour. Then add mushrooms, and cook together gently for a few minutes without browning. Add 1 cup of heated cream and the Sherry. Salt and pepper to taste. Cook a little longer, until mixture thickens.

For the Cream Sauce:

1 recipe white sauce
Parmesan cheese
Paprika

Spread pancakes with lobster filling, roll, and place in greased baking dish. Pour cream sauce over all, sprinkle with Parmesan cheese and paprika, broil lightly, and serve immediately. Serves 6.

LOBSTER NEWBURG

4 cups boiled lobster meat
Salt, pepper, pakrika
2 pints heavy cream
1 pony glass Cognac
1 cup Sherry
5 ounces butter

Season the lobster pieces with salt, white pepper and paprika. Melt 2 ounces of the butter in a saucepan and fry the lobster pieces gently about 2 minutes. Add the Cognac and the Sherry. Let it simmer until liquid is halfway reduced. Add cream. Let it simmer again until it reaches a nice creamy consistency. Add the remaining butter (do not allow the lobster to boil while adding the butter). Adjust seasoning. Serve the Lobster Newburg with freshly made toast, cut into triangles. Serves 8-10.

LOBSTER À LA MARSEILLES

1 lobster (1½ pounds)
1 tablespoon butter
1 finely chopped small onion
6 large mushrooms
Salt, pepper
1½ cups canned tomatoes
Parsley

Boil or steam lobster; remove meat from shell and cut into small cubes. Add butter, onion, finely chopped mushroom stems, seasonings and lobster meat to 1 cup stewed tomatoes and simmer 3 to 4 minutes; turn into casserole. Peel and sauté mushroom caps and place on lobster. Pour remaining ½ cup tomatoes over top and bake in 350° oven 10 minutes. Garnish with parsley. Serves 4.

SEAFOOD AND PASTA CASSEROLE

2 cups medium pasta shells
½ cup butter
1 lb. raw cleaned shrimp, cut butterfly style
3 cloves garlic, crushed
4 small onions, grated
1½ tablespoons oregano
2 tablespoons flour
2 pimentos, chopped
½ cup parsley, chopped
1 (6-oz.) can minced clams
1 (8-oz.) jar clam juice
2 (7-oz.) pkgs. frozen king crab meat
¼ cup grated Parmesan cheese

Cook shells until tender. Rinse in cold, then hot water. Add ¼ cup butter and toss till coated. While shells are boiling, cook in remaining butter for five minutes the shrimp, garlic, onions, oregano, flour, half of pimento and parsley. Remove from heat. Reserve a few shrimp for garnish. Add to mixture clams with their juice, bottled clam juice and separated pieces of crab. Arrange alternate layers of pasta and cooked mixture in greased 2-quart casserole. Sprinkle each layer with cheese. Garnish with remaining pimento and shrimp. Cover with foil. Refrigerate. Near serving time let come to room tem-

perature, bake 20 minutes at 300°, till heated through. Serves 8.

SEA FOOD MORNAY

6 tablespoons butter
½ cup onion, finely minced
1 scallion, thinly sliced
1 clove garlic, finely minced
6 tablespoons flour
3 cups milk
1 cup heavy cream
Salt and pepper
2 cups mushrooms, thinly sliced
1 cup fresh bay scallops
2 cups sharp Cheddar cheese, grated
1 cup cooked shrimp, shelled and deveined
1 cup cooked lobster, cut into bite-size pieces
1 cup lump crab meat
2 tablespoons dry Sherry
2 hard-boiled eggs, quartered
6 patty shells.

Melt butter in a saucepan and cook onion, scallion and garlic, stirring frequently, until onion is light gold in color. Sprinkle with flour and add milk, stirring rapidly. Add cream and cook, stirring, until mixture is thickened and smooth. Simmer, stirring frequently, 10 minutes or longer. Season with salt and pepper.

Meanwhile, heat two tablespoons butter and cook mushrooms until they are wilted. Continue cooking, shaking skillet, until most of moisture evaporates.

Place scallops in a saucepan and add salted water to cover. Bring to a boil and simmer gently five minutes. Remove from heat and drain.

Remove cream sauce from heat and stir in cheese. Stir until cheese melts. Add scallops, mushrooms, shrimp, lobster and crab to sauce. If necessary, season with salt and pepper. Stir in Sherry and hard-boiled eggs.

Spoon mixture into patty shells and bake 10 minutes in 400° oven. Serves 6.

PARTAN BREE

4 cups milk
¼ cup quick-cooking rice
2 envelopes chicken broth or
   2 chicken bouillon cubes
1 tablespoon anchovy paste
1 cup cooked crabmeat or
   1 (7-oz.) can crabmeat, drained
½ cup heavy cream

Combine milk, quick-cooking rice, and chicken broth with 1 tablespoon anchovy paste, in a medium saucepan. Bring to a boil. Remove from heat, cover and let stand 10 minutes. Add crabmeat, drained, and heavy cream.

Reheat soup slowly, stirring constantly. *Do not boil.* Serves 6.

FISH PUDDING

5 pounds haddock
¾ cup rice
2 cups water
2 cups milk
1 teaspoon salt
4 eggs, well-beaten
5 cups milk
Butter, salt, pepper

Boil fish in salted water about 45 minutes, or until tender. Drain, skin carefully, pick out bones, and flake finely. Cook rice with water, milk and salt for 20 minutes. Now put a layer of drained rice in a 3-quart casserole. Add a layer of the fish. Season with butter, pepper and salt. Continue with alternate layers until casserole is two-thirds full. To well-beaten eggs add milk. Pour over rice and fish. Bake uncovered for 1 hour in a 350° oven. Serves 12.

CONTENTS